FIRST READERS

Jeremy Taylor

The Secret of the Lost Dogs

VERLAG MORITZ DIESTERWEG
Frankfurt am Main

Neue Rechtschreibung

ISBN 3-425-03060-4

Illustrationen: Ulf Marckwort, Kassel
Satz und Reproduktion: graphoprint, Koblenz
Druck und Bindung: Weihert-Druck, Darmstadt

Printed in Germany

CHAPTER ONE

It was the most important football match in the world. **Hendon**[1] United were playing against the **Notting Hill**[2] Allstars. It was a hot Saturday afternoon and there were only two minutes before the end of the game.

"**Pass**[3], Vera! Quickly!" shouted Charlie.

Vera passed the ball to Charlie. Charlie ran forward and kicked the ball at the **goal.**[4] "Yes!"

"No!" shouted Susan who was playing in goal for the Notting Hill team. She jumped like a cat and caught the ball.

Both[5] teams were playing well. It was still 2-2. Susan **threw**[6] the ball to Gillian. Vera stood in front of her. "Pass, Gillian!" shouted Karim.

Gillian passed to Karim and **ran**[7] **past**[8] Vera. Karim controlled the ball then passed it quickly back to Gillian. She ran forward. David was the **goalkeeper**[9] for Hendon United. Gillian knew he was good, but was he good enough? Gillian shot. David jumped to his right. But the ball went past his fingers.

"Yes!" shouted Gillian.

"No!" shouted David.

[1]**Hendon**/[2]**Notting Hill** Stadtteile im N-O Londons [3]**to pass (the ball)** (den Ball) zuspielen [4]**goal** (*Sport*) Tor [5]**both** beide [6]**to throw** [θrəʊ] **(threw** [θru:], **thrown)** (*hier*) zuwerfen [7]**to run (ran, run)** rennen [8]**past** hinter [9]**goalkeeper** Torwart

"Aaaaargh!" shouted an old lady. The ball **flew**[1] over the goal and **hit**[2] the old lady's head. But what was an old lady doing behind the goal of the most important football match in the world?

"I'm very sorry," said Gillian to the old lady. "I didn't see you. I was looking at the goal."

"That's okay," said the old lady, but Gillian saw that she was crying.

"**We are sorry**[3]," said David and put his arm around the old lady. "We …"

"I'm not crying because of your football," said the old lady.

"No?" said David. "So, why are you crying?"

[1]**to fly (flew, flown)** fliegen [2]**to hit** treffen [3]**we are sorry** es tut uns Leid

"I'm crying because of Flopper."

"Flopper? Who is Flopper?"

"My cocker spaniel. Every day we walk around the park together." The old lady stopped and **blew her nose.**[1] "Today, I was talking to a friend of mine. When I looked up, Flopper wasn't there."

"Don't worry," said Gillian. "We'll help you to find Flopper. Come on, guys! The football match can wait. Let's help this lady find Flopper."

"Oh, thank you so much," said the old lady.

"Wait a minute!" shouted Charlie. "Is that Flopper?"

Charlie **pointed at**[2] a man and a woman with a dog. They were running out of the park. The man had a dog in his arms.

"I can't see from here," said the old lady. "What colour is the dog?"

"He's small and brown," said Karim. "Do you think it's Flopper?"

"Yes, that's him!" shouted the old lady.

Suddenly,[3] all the football players were running across the park. "We must stop them!" shouted Charlie.

At the side of the park, the man and the woman with the dog jumped into a car. "Stop!" shouted Gillian.

But the man in the car didn't listen to Gillian. He looked back and saw the children just ten metres away from his car.

[1]**to blow (blew, blown) one's nose** sich die Nase putzen [2]**to point at** zeigen, deuten [3]**suddenly** plötzlich

Then he put his foot down on the gas pedal and **drove away**[1] very quickly.

"We nearly stopped him," said Vera. "Did anyone get the **registration number**[2] of the car?"

"I think it was 'C419TPO'," said David.

"I thought it was 'C491PTO'," said Gillian.

"So, what are we going to do now?" asked Charlie.

"We can go to the police," said Susan.

"But what can we tell them?" asked Karim. "We don't know the registration number of the car. We don't know the name of the old lady. We only know the name of the dog!"

"And what about our game of football?" asked David. "I'm sure that Hendon United were going to win."

"Forget football for the moment, David," said Gillian. "Let's try and help the old lady. She will be happy – and it will be an adventure for us."

"Like detectives!" said Vera.

"Okay, let's go to Joe's Snackbar and have a milkshake and make plans," said David.

So, David, Karim, Susan, Gillian, Vera and Charlie went to Joe's Snackbar for seven milkshakes (Gillian always has two) and to make plans …

[1]**to drive (drove, driven) away** davonfahren [2]**registration number** Kennzeichen

CHAPTER TWO

There were a lot of people in Joe's Snackbar. The children **stood around**[1] for a moment and then **sat down**[2] in the middle of a long table. At one end of the table was a **homeless**[3] woman called Bessie. She was wearing a heavy brown coat. Outside, it was twenty six degrees Celsius. (Yes, sometimes even London has good weather!) Bessie was drinking a cup of tea very slowly. At the other end of the table were three boys. Each of the boys ate one of Joe's special burgers, a super mega burger with a 400 gram burger inside. The boys were eating as fast as possible!

"So what are we going to do?" asked Karim.
"We can go to the police," said Susan.

[1]**to stand (stood, stood) around** herumstehen [2]**to sit (sat, sat) down** sich hinsetzen [3]**homeless** obdachlos

"But we don't have enough information," said Charlie.

"Well, what do we know at the moment?" asked Gillian. She **took out**[1] a little red book and pen from the pocket of her jacket.

"An old lady lost her dog, called Flopper," said Vera.

"Dog, called Flopper," repeated Detective Gillian, writing the information into her book.

"And we saw two people. A man and a woman, running away with Flopper," said Susan.

"Are we sure that it was Flopper?" asked Gillian.

"No, not one hundred per cent," said Charlie, "but maybe ninety per cent."

"Ninety per cent sure," repeated Gillian. "Now, what did the man look like?"

"He was tall, black and he had a **beard**[2]," said Karim. "He was **probably**[3] about forty."

"And what about the woman? What did she look like?"

"She was younger," said Vera. "She was probably about twenty five. She had blonde hair, a bit like Susan's hair."

"Okay, and what about the dog, Flopper? Did anyone see Flopper? Charlie, you were next to the car when the man drove away. Did you see Flopper?"

"I saw him," said Charlie. "He was a cocker spaniel, brown with long ears, and ..."

"What is it, Charlie?"

"I'm not sure, but I think I saw blood on his leg."

[1]**to take out** herausholen [2]**beard** Bart [3]**probably** wahrscheinlich

"Blood?" whispered David. "Please don't talk about blood. When I think…about…it…I…sometimes…"

"David, are you okay, David?" asked Gillian.

David didn't answer. He was in a different world.

"Don't worry about David," said Susan. "He hates blood. Every time he sees it – or even thinks about it, he **faints**[1]."

"Are you looking for a dog?" asked Bessie.

"That's right," said Charlie.

"Go to the dogs' home. They've got lots of dogs there."

"We don't want a dog," answered Charlie. "We are trying to help an old lady. She has lost her dog."

"If she wants to find her dog, she should put a postcard in the post office," said one of the boys with a mega burger. "If she offers a **reward**[2], someone will find her dog."

"But we saw two people," said Gillian. "They **stole**[3] the dog."

"What do these people look like?" asked Bessie.

Gillian looked at her little red book. "The man was tall, black, he had a beard, and he was about forty."

"And the woman," said Bessie, "was she white, about thirty with long blonde hair?"

"Yes, how did you know?" asked Gillian.

"I just saw them walk past the snack bar," said Bessie very **calmly**[4].

"Really?" asked Karim. "Come on everybody, let's go and **rescue**[5] Flopper!"

[1]**to faint** ohnmächtig werden [2]**reward** Belohnung [3]**to steal (stole, stolen)** stehlen [4]**calmly** ruhig, beruhigend [5]**to rescue** retten

"Er, Karim, you've forgotten David," said Susan. "I'll stay here with him. I'll call you later."

"I...don't...like...blood...I...want...a...milkshake," **whispered**[1] David. Then he went back to sleep on Susan's **shoulder**[2].

CHAPTER THREE

"There they are!" whispered Gillian. "Outside the **library**[3]. And there's Flopper with a **bandage**[4] around his leg."

"But how can we rescue Flopper?" asked Charlie.

"There's only one way," said Vera. "We must steal Flopper. They stole Flopper. We can steal him back."

"But how?" asked Charlie.

"I have a plan," said Karim. "Now listen to me carefully..."

"That's a lovely dog," said Karim.

"Thank you," said the woman with the blonde hair.

"He's a cocker spaniel, isn't he?"

"That's right," answered the woman. "His name's Sponker. Are you interested in dogs?"

"Hello Sponker," said Karim and scratched Sponker behind his ears. "Er, yes, I want a dog **of my own**[5]."

"Well if you go to the dogs' home," said the man with the beard, "they have got a lot of beautiful dogs there."

[1]**to whisper** flüstern [2]**shoulder** Schulter [3]**library** Bibliothek, Bücherei [4]**bandage** Verband [5]**... of my own** eigen

"Is that where you got Flop … Sponker?" asked Karim.

"No, we bought him two …"

"Help! Someone! Please help!" A girl was **lying**[1] on the **pavement**[2]. "My **ankle**[3] is killing me!"

The tall man with the beard ran to her. "I'm a doctor. Are you okay? What happened?"

"I was running and then I **fell over**[4]," said the girl, trying to cry.

"Can you …"

"Stop **thief**[5]! John!" shouted the woman. "That boy has stolen Sponker!"

"Which way did he go?"

"That way!"

[1]**to lie (lay, lain)** liegen [2]**pavement** Bürgersteig [3]**ankle** Fußgelenk, Knöchel [4]**to fall (fell, fallen) over** hinfallen [5]**thief** Dieb

The man with the beard ran to the end of the street but he had no chance. There were so many people. He went back to his wife. "I don't understand this. I was helping the girl on the ground and … wait a minute, where is she now?"

The girl – Vera – was now running as fast as possible. (Her ankle was perfect again!) Outside Joe's Snackbar she met Karim and Gillian. Charlie was inside talking to Susan and David. "Where's Flopper?"

"In my bag," said Gillian.

Vera looked down. Flopper looked up and **barked**[1]. "Don't worry, Flopper. We are going to take you home," said Vera.

"Woof woof!" barked Flopper.

"Okay, David's feeling much better now," said Charlie.

"Let's take Flopper back to the park. **Hopefully**[2] we'll find the old lady again."

Gillian, Vera, Karim and Charlie walked quickly back to the park. "There she is!" shouted Karim.

And there she was. The old lady was still looking for her dog. But now, thanks to the detectives, she was going to be a very happy old lady …

"Hello, do you remember us?" asked Charlie.

"Yes, you're the children with the football, aren't you?"

"That's right," said Gillian. "But we have a **surprise**[3] for you!"

[1]**to bark** bellen [2]**hopefully** hoffentlich [3]**surprise** Überraschung

"A surprise?" said the old lady.

"We found Flopper!" said Charlie proudly.

"Really? My Flopper? Where is he?"

"Woof woof!" barked Flopper.

"Here he is," said Gillian and lifted Flopper out of her bag.

"Hello, Flo ..." The old lady stopped.

"What's wrong?" asked Vera.

"That isn't Flopper!"

"It must be," said Charlie. "We saw two people in the park **earlier**[1]. They ran away from us with Flopper. Don't you remember?"

"I remember," said the old lady. "But the dog that they ran away with, was not Flopper."

"Oh no!" said Vera.

"Oh dear!" said Charlie.

"Oh dear, oh dear!" said Gillian.

"Oh dear, oh dear, oh dear!" said Karim.

"Woof woof," barked Sponker.

"One more thing," said Gillian. "A boy in Joe's Snackbar had a good idea. You can put an **advertisement**[2] in the window of the post office. Perhaps someone has found Flopper. Perhaps you can **offer**[3] a reward."

"That's a good idea," said the old lady. "I'll go to the post office now before it closes."

[1]**early (earlier, earliest)** früh [2]**advertisement** Anzeige [3]**to offer** anbieten

CHAPTER FOUR

Twenty minutes later, Gillian, Charlie, Vera and Karim were back in Joe's Snackbar.

"Hi, guys!" said David. "So did you give Flopper back to the old lady?"

"Er, yes and no," said Charlie.

"What do you mean, yes and no?" asked Susan.

"Well, we gave her the dog – but it wasn't her dog," said Karim.

"What?!" said Susan and David together.

"You mean, you stole the wrong dog?"

"That's right," said Vera. "We wanted to help the old lady but now we have an even bigger problem!"

"So where is the new dog?" asked Susan.

"You mean Sponker?" asked Gillian. "He's here, in my bag."

"Woof woof," barked Sponker, when he heard his name.

"What was that?" shouted Joe. "I don't want any animals in my bar."

"Er, don't worry, Joe," said Gillian. "It was only Charlie – barking like a dog."

"Woof woof!" barked Charlie.

Joe looked at Gillian and Charlie and then went back to his work.

"Okay, we've got two problems," said Gillian. "Problem number one, we have a dog and we have to find the **owners**[1]

[1]**owner** Besitzer

of the dog. Problem number two, we have an old lady, Mrs. Baxter, who has lost her dog. I wrote her telephone number down so we can call her. So now, problem number one, how are we going to find the owners of S-P-O-N-K-E-R?"

"When I was lying on the floor," said Vera, "the man said he is a doctor."

"And I heard the woman call him 'John'," said Karim.

"A doctor called 'John'," said Gillian. "There must be a million doctors in London called John."

"But not in Notting Hill," said Charlie. "We can look in the telephone book. Perhaps there are only a few."

"Good idea, Charlie," said Gillian. "Joe, please can I look at the telephone book?"

"What for?" asked Joe.

"I need to find a doctor," said Gillian.

"Mmm, I think you all need a special kind of doctor," said Joe. But after two minutes he gave Gillian **a book of local businesses and services**[1].

"Thanks a lot, Joe," said Gillian.

Ten minutes later, they had the names of eighteen local doctors called John.

"So what are we going to do now?" asked Vera.

"Well, I stole S-P-O-N-K-E-R," said Karim, "so I think I must make the telephone calls."

"I'll come with you," said Susan.

"Okay, let's meet tonight and we can make some more plans."

[1]**a book of local businesses and services** (*etwa*) Gelbe Seiten

"Why don't you all come to my flat?" said Charlie. "About seven o'clock?"

"We'll be there," said Gillian.

CHAPTER FIVE

Karim and Susan **left**[1] Joe's Snackbar and went to the library. Susan **held**[2] Gillian's bag with Sponker. She waited outside. Karim went inside and found a telephone. He took out his **phonecard**[3] and the piece of paper with the telephone numbers. He pushed his phonecard into the telephone and called the first number.

"Doctor Adams' **surgery**[4], can I help you?"

"I hope so. Has Doctor Adams got a dog called Sponker?"

"What?"

"I know this is not a normal question, but I stole a dog today and I know the owner is a local doctor called John."

"Mmm, I think I understand."

"So?"

"So what?"

"So has Doctor Adams got a dog called Sponker?"

"I don't think so. He hates dogs. He's got a cat called Tinkerbell. She's a lovely little thing. She's almost all black but she has white ears and ..."

[1]**to leave (left, left)** verlassen [2]**to hold (held, held)** halten [3]**phonecard** Telefonkarte [4]**surgery** Sprechzimmer/Praxis

"That's very interesting but I must find the owner of Sponker."

"Oh, okay, goodbye."

"Goodbye, and thank you for your time," said Karim. He put down the phone and then picked it up again. 'One down, seventeen to go' thought Karim.

After forty five minutes, Karim came out of the library. He walked slowly and he wasn't smiling. "No luck?" said Susan.

"Not yet," said Karim, "but I've only called eleven doctors so far. Everybody thinks I'm crazy."

"Well, I think the situation is a little crazy," said Susan. "You stole a dog that you didn't want to steal."

"So do you think I'm crazy as well?"

"Just a little, Karim."

"Woof woof!" barked Sponker.

"Thanks a lot, Susan and Sponker. Okay, what time is it?"

"Half past five,"

"I'll call my mum and tell her I won't be home for tea. Then I'll call the other doctors."

Karim went back into the library. He put his phonecard back into the phone, called his mum and then called doctor number twelve.

After number twelve came numbers thirteen, fourteen and then, at five to six, a librarian told him he had five minutes.

Quickly, he called doctor number fifteen.

"Hello, Doctor Underhill's surgery. Can I help you?"

"Yes, I have an **unusual**[1] question. Can you tell me if Doctor Underhill is black?"

"Yes, he is. Why do you want to know?"

"That's great. Do you know if Doctor Underhill has got a dog?"

"I'm sorry, I don't know that. I'm new here. Why don't you call back tomorrow?"

"This is very important. Is Doctor Underhill there at the moment?"

"Well, yes he is, but he's in a very bad **mood**[2] today. I don't know why."

"I think I do," said Karim. "I think I stole his dog today."

"You did what?!"

"I stole his dog. I ..."

"What a terrible thing to do!" The woman stopped talking to Karim. Karim listened very carefully and he could hear her talking with the doctor. "Ah, Doctor Underhill ... Yes, there's a boy on the telephone. He says he stole your dog."

Suddenly, Karim heard a man's voice on the telephone.

"Hello, this is Doctor John Underhill speaking."

"Hello, my name is Karim Khan. I think I stole your dog today."

"You think you stole it? Don't you know?" asked Doctor Underhill.

"Are you the owner of Sponker?"

[1]**unusual** ungewöhnlich [2]**mood** Laune

"I am."

"Oh that's great. Well, we have him here. He's safe."

"Oh, I think I understand," said Doctor Underhill. The doctor liked to read a lot of books about crime and detectives. "Okay, how much do you want?"

"I'm sorry?" said Karim.

"How much do you want – for Sponker?"

Suddenly Karim understood. "No, no, Doctor Underhill. You don't understand. I didn't want to steal Sponker."

"You didn't?"

"No, it was a mistake."

"Mmm," said the doctor. "So you stole Sponker, shall we say, **accidentally**[1]?"

"Yes, well no. I wanted to steal another dog called Flopper," said Karim.

Poor Doctor Underhill did not know what to believe! "Look this is all getting very **complicated**[2]," said the doctor. "Can I see you tonight and take Sponker home?"

"Yes, of course," said Karim. "We are going to meet at Charlie's flat."

Karim gave Charlie's address to the doctor and finally left the library. Outside the library, Susan was reading a book. Sponker was sleeping next to her. "Hi, Karim, did you ...?"

Karim didn't need to answer. The big smile on his face told Susan the answer she wanted to hear. "That's great!" she said, "now we only have to find Flopper!"

[1] **accidentally** zufällig, versehentlich   [2] **complicated** kompliziert, schwierig

CHAPTER SIX

Karim bought some Indian **samosas**[1] from an Indian **take away**[2]. "Would you like one?"

"Woof! Woof!" barked Sponker.

Karim laughed. "Okay, Sponker. I didn't forget you. I'm sure you're hungry. Would you like to try an Indian samosa?"

"Woof! Woof!" barked Sponker again.

Karim understood him perfectly. "Okay, here you are, Sponker."

Sponker ate the samosa very quickly and then looked to Karim for more. "Sorry, Sponker, no more."

"What kind are they?" asked Susan.

"These two are meat and those three are vegetable."

"Thanks," said Susan. She took one of the vegetable samosas and bit into it. "Mmmm, it's delicious! Indian food is much better than English food."

"I like both," said Karim. "And have you ever eaten West Indian food?"

"No, not yet," answered Susan.

"Charlie's mum is an excellent cook. I had dinner at their flat **a couple of weeks ago**[3]."

Susan, Karim and Sponker sat in the park and ate their samosas. At ten to seven, they walked up the street to Charlie's flat.

"Karim! It's nice to see you again!"

[1]**samosa** (eine indische Speise) [2]**take away** (eine Art Imbissstand mit Gerichten zum Mitnehmen) [3]**a couple of weeks ago** vor einigen Wochen

"Hello, Mrs. Macintosh, you're looking well."

"I haven't got time to be ill, Karim. I need all the time I have to look after Charlie and his sisters."

Karim laughed. He liked Mrs. Macintosh. She was a friendly woman and also a great cook! Karim and Susan **knocked**[1] on Charlie's bedroom door.

"Come in!"

Karim, Susan and Sponker went into Charlie's bedroom. It was not a very big bedroom. So it was very **crowded**[2] with Charlie and his friends – and don't forget Wanda, Charlie's goldfish. She lives in a bowl on Charlie's desk.

"So, what's new?" asked Charlie.

Karim and Susan sat down on Charlie's bed. Karim told everyone about the phone calls that he made.

"So, the doctor is coming here?" asked Vera.

"That's right," said Susan. "About half past seven."

Vera looked at her watch. It was twenty past seven.

Another ten minutes …

At exactly half past seven there was a knock on Charlie's door. "It's the doctor!" said David.

But it wasn't. It was Mrs. Macintosh with a big **tray**[3] of drinks and a big plate full of **home-made**[4] cakes.

"Wow!" said everyone.

"Woof woof!" barked Sponker.

"What is that dog doing in here?" asked Mrs. Macintosh.

[1]**to knock** klopfen [2]**crowded** voll, überfüllt [3]**tray** Tablett [4]**home-made** selbstgemacht

Charlie and Karim looked at each other. They didn't know what to say. "Er, Karim found him," said Gillian.

"Found him?" said Mrs. Macintosh.

"Er, yes, I found him," said Karim. "I was outside the library with Susan and we saw the dog. His name's Sponker."

"Woof woof!" barked Sponker.

"He looked very sad," said Susan. "So we took him and then we telephoned his owner."

"Mmmm," said Mrs. Macintosh. She knew something was not right but she didn't know what it was.

Two minutes later, Mrs. Macintosh was back. "Charlie, you have a visitor."

"Doctor Underhill!" said Karim.

Charlie left his bedroom with Sponker. In the living-room was the tall man with a beard. "Woof woof!" barked Sponker.

"Doctor Underhill?" asked Charlie. Charlie remembered the man. He was the same man who had run across the park with the dog in his arms.

"That's right. And you must be Charlie Macintosh."

"That's right," said Charlie.

"Would you like a cup of tea, Doctor Underhill?" asked Mrs. Macintosh.

"No, thank you. I'm not staying," said the doctor.

"We're sorry," said Charlie. "We really are very sorry. We didn't want to steal Sponker."

"But you and your **gang**[1] do steal dogs, don't you?" said the doctor.

"No!" said Charlie. "We only wanted to help an old lady. "She lost her dog. We … we …"

"Yes?"

"We thought you and your friend stole the old lady's dog."

"You thought my wife and I stole Sponker? Why!?" asked the doctor a little angrily.

"We saw you in the park. We saw you running away with Sponker. We thought it was Flopper – the old lady's dog. So, why were you running?"

"We were running," said the doctor, "because Sponker cut his foot on a piece of glass. We had to take him to a **vet**[2]."

"Oh!" said Charlie. "Now I understand."

[1]**gang** Bande [2]**vet** Tierarzt

"I saw you and your friends **chasing**[1] us. We were worried. We thought you wanted to **attack**[2] us!"

"Attack you? No, no, no," said Charlie. "We only wanted to help an old lady."

For the first time that day, Doctor John Underhill smiled. "I read a book when I was a boy. It was about some people who stole animals. The people took the animals and then waited for a reward."

"It sounds like a good story," said Charlie. "How did the story end?"

Doctor Underhill thought. "I'm sorry, it was a very long time ago. I can't remember it now."

After a few more minutes, Doctor Underhill said goodbye to Charlie and to Mrs. Macintosh and left the flat with Sponker.

"Goodbye, Sponker!" called Charlie.

"Woof woof!" barked Sponker.

CHAPTER SEVEN

Charlie went back to his friends in his bedroom.

"And?"

"What did he say?"

"Was he angry?"

"Is he going to call the police?"

Charlie smiled. "He understood our mistake. But he was worried."

[1]**to chase** jagen, verfolgen [2]**to attack** angreifen

"Worried? Why?" asked Vera.

"He read a book when he was a boy. It was about some people who stole animals. Then they waited for a reward."

"That's terrible," said Susan. "What happened to them? Did the police catch them?"

"The doctor didn't remember. He said it ..."

Suddenly Gillian jumped up. Then she sat down again. Then she jumped up again.

"Er, Gillian," said Karim. "I know Mrs. Macintosh's cakes are good. But why are you so excited?"

"I've got it!" shouted Gillian.

"Er, what have you got?" asked David.

"The answer! Do you remember the boys we saw in Joe's Snackbar?"

"Do you mean the tall one with blond hair and the two short boys with brown hair?" asked Karim. "I know the tall boy. His name is Paul Fisher. He's in my class at school."

"Do you remember what they said to us?" asked Gillian.

"Something about a reward," said Vera.

"Exactly!" said Gillian and jumped up and down again.

"Do you think that the boys ..." said Charlie.

"I don't only think," said Gillian. "I know! I'm **positive**[1], one hundred per cent."

"Perhaps you're right," said David. "But what can we do?"

"Listen to me," said Gillian. "I've got a plan ..."

[1]**to be positive** sicher sein

CHAPTER EIGHT

The next day was a Sunday. It was half past nine in the morning. Gillian and Karim were in the park. They weren't playing football or cricket. They were hiding in some bushes at the side of the park.

"I'm hungry," said Karim. "Are you sure that ..."

"Shhhh!" whispered Gillian.

"What is it?" asked Karim.

Someone was walking near the bushes. Karim and Gillian looked out from the bushes very carefully. "It's ..."

"Mrs. Baxter!" said Gillian. "And she's got a dog with her. Come on, Karim!"

"Hello, Mrs. Baxter."

"Oh, hello."

"Is that Flopper?" asked Karim.

"Yes, it is," said Mrs. Baxter. "It was a good idea you gave me. I put an advertisement in the window of the post office. One hour later a very kind boy came to my flat. He found Flopper in the street. Of course, I gave him a reward. Do you think five pounds was enough?"

"Yes, I am sure five pounds was more than enough, Mrs. Baxter," said Gillian. "What did the boy look like?"

"He was quite tall and had blond hair. Quite a good looking boy. It's nice to know that there are some kind people in Notting Hill."

"Okay, Mrs. Baxter," said Karim. "We have to go. Look after Flopper!"

"I will, don't worry," said Mrs. Baxter and threw a ball across the park. Flopper ran after it.

"Come on, Karim. Let's get back to the bushes and wait."

At ten o'clock, David and Susan **met**[1] Karim and Gillian.

"Hi, how is it going?" asked Susan.

"We saw Mrs. Baxter," said Karim. "Someone 'found' Flopper."

"Was it one of the boys?" asked David.

"Mrs. Baxter said that the boy was tall, had blond hair and was good looking."

"Mmm," said Susan. "I don't think the blond boy in Joe's Snackbar was good looking."

"Don't forget," said Gillian. "Mrs. Baxter **wears** thick **glasses!**[2]"

Susan laughed. "Perhaps ..."

"What is it, Susan?" asked Karim.

"Look!"

Karim, David and Gillian looked. It was the boys from Joe's Snackbar! They were coming in the direction of the bushes. One of them was carrying a red rucksack. "Quick, hide!" whispered Gillian.

[1]**to meet (met, met)** treffen [2]**to wear glasses** eine Brille tragen

The boys walked very close to Karim. One boy **stepped**[1] on Karim's foot but (luckily) Karim didn't shout. The boys walked through a **gap**[2] in the bushes and left the park.

"That was close!" said Karim.

"Did you hear it?" asked Gillian.

"Hear what?" asked David.

"A dog," answered Gillian. "It was in the red rucksack."

"Well done, Gillian," said Karim. "You were right about the boys. But what are we going to do now?"

"I don't know," said Gillian. "We need a new plan."

Gillian, Karim, David and Susan were thinking of a new plan. Suddenly they heard a man shouting. "Bonzo! Come on Bonzo! Where are you?"

[1]**to step** treten [2]**gap** Lücke

"I think we know where Bonzo is," said Gillian. "Come on, let's help the man."

"Have you seen my dog? His name's Bonzo and he's a Yorkshire terrier," said the man.

"I can help you find him," said Karim.

"You can?" said the man. "How?"

"Just wait," said Karim. He sat down and crossed his legs. Then he put his hands together and closed his eyes.

"What's he doing?" asked the man. "Is he in a **trance**[1]?"

"Yes," whispered Gillian.

"Bonzo? Can you hear me Bonzo?" said Karim in a very strange voice. "Okay, Bonzo, I can hear you. Where are you? ...Okay, Bonzo, I will come and help you."

Karim stood up very slowly. He put his hands in front of him and walked – a bit like a robot. He walked through

[1]**trance** Trance(zustand)

the gap in the bushes. David, Susan, Gillian and the man followed him.

He walked down the street next to the park. Many people looked at him and pointed at him. But Karim just walked. Finally he turned into a small house with an **untidy**[1] garden. He sat down in front of the door.

"But this is crazy! Bonzo isn't here," said the man.

"Let's ring the bell and find out," said Gillian.

A woman opened the door. "Yes?"

"Um, er, well, this may be a strange question," said the man. "But, well, you see, I've lost my dog, and, well, I was wondering, if, perhaps, you've seen him?"

"Is he a Yorkshire terrier?" asked the woman.

"Yes, that's right," said the man.

"You're very lucky," said the woman. "My son found him in the street about ten minutes ago. You're lucky your dog is still alive."

The woman went inside and got Bonzo. "There you are," she said. "And what about a reward for my son? He **saved**[2] your dog."

"Yes, of course," said the man. "Here's ten pounds."

"Thanks," said the woman and closed the door.

"You," said the man, "have a great talent!"

"Thanks a lot," said Karim.

"But I must give you a reward as well," said the man.

"I cannot take money from you," said Karim very seriously. "Now, we must go."

[1]**untidy** unordentlich [2]**to save** retten

Karim, David, Gillian and Susan left the man and walked to Joe's Snackbar. When they got there they met Charlie and Vera. Charlie and Vera laughed when Susan told them about Karim's 'trance'. "So now we are sure it is those boys," said Gillian. "They steal dogs and wait for a reward."

"Perhaps they will try and steal Wanda!" said Charlie.

Gillian smiled. "You're right, Charlie. Don't take Wanda for a walk in the park!"

"But seriously," said Vera. "What are we going to do?"

Charlie, Gillian, David, Vera, Karim and Susan tried to think of a new plan. After ten minutes (and seven milkshakes) Charlie jumped up. "I've got it!"

"A plan?" asked Susan.

"The best plan in the world!" said Charlie. "Now listen to me carefully ..."

CHAPTER NINE

Ten minutes later, Charlie was outside his neighbour's house. His neighbour is a **magician**[1]! Charlie rang the bell and waited.

"Hello, Charlie. Come in!"

Charlie went in.

"Cup of tea?"

"Please," said Charlie. "Milk, no sugar."

Charlie was sitting in the living-room. There were so many interesting things in the room. It was always fascinating for

[1]**magician** Zauberer

him to see the talking **parrot**[1] and the beautiful white rabbit. There were a lot of pictures of magicians on the walls. They were all looking at Charlie. He was actually a little bit nervous.

"Here you are, Charlie."

"Thanks a lot."

The magician sat down and listened to Charlie's plan.

"I'm not sure," he said at the end. "I'm very busy at the moment. I have a show at four o'clock. I don't really have time."

"Oh, please. It's very important," said Charlie.

"Okay, Charlie. I'll do it."

"You *and* Percy?"

"Yes, me *and* Percy," said the magician.

"Thanks a lot!" said Charlie. "You're the best neighbour in the world!"

CHAPTER TEN

There were a lot of people in the park that afternoon. Some young people were playing **frisbee**[2]. Some old men were playing **bowls**[3]. A family were flying a model plane. But Charlie and his friends were not in the park. They were in Vera's mum's office next to the park. It was on the fourth floor. They were watching Charlie's neighbour. He was in the park near some bushes. He was looking for something in the grass. Suddenly a boy came up to him.

[1]**parrot** Papagei [2]**frisbee** Frisbee(scheibe) [3]**bowls** Boccia

"What have you lost?" asked the boy.

"I've lost Percy!" said the magician

"Oh, is Percy a little black and white collie?"

"No."

"Is he **a golden retriever**[1] **puppy**[2]?"

"No."

"So what kind of dog is Percy?"

"Percy isn't a dog. Percy is my python. I was walking with ..."

"A p..p..python?"

"Yes, I think he went into those bushes over there."

"O...o...over th..th..there?"

"Yes, is there anything wrong?" said the magician

"N..n..no, no, e..e..everything's f..f..fine," said the boy.

The boy ran quickly back to the bushes. "Hey guys, look out! There's a **snake**[3] in the bushes, a python!"

"A python?" said Paul Fisher, the tall boy with blond hair. "Don't be crazy. It's not April the First."

"Well that man over there told me he has lost his pet python called Percy."

"Ha ha, very funny. Now be quiet and look out for a young woman. She is trying to find her golden retriever."

Nervously, the boy joined his friends.

After two minutes, one boy said, "Stop that!"

"Stop what?"

"Stop touching my leg!"

[1]**golden retriever** (*Hunderasse*) Golden Retriever [2]**puppy** junger Hund [3]**snake** Schlange

"I didn't ."

"You did."

"**Honestly**[1], I didn't."

"Then if you didn't …"

"Aaaaaaaaaargh!"

Charlie and his friends watched as the three boys ran out of the bushes. They ran out of the park. The tall boy with the blond hair had his red rucksack. There were two dogs in the rucksack, a small collie and a golden retriever puppy.

"Your plan was quite good," said Gillian. "But the boys are going to **escape**[2]."

"No they won't," said Charlie. "Watch carefully."

Charlie's friends watched the three boys. Suddenly, two policemen jumped out of a car and stopped the boys.

"How did you do it, Charlie?"

"With a little help from my friends," said Charlie.

"But what about the police?" asked Karim.

"A friend of mine knows the Chief Inspector," said Charlie.

"A friend of yours?" asked Vera. "Who?"

"Look down there!" said Charlie.

Everybody looked. Next to the police car was a man. He was a tall man and he had a beard. He had a small dog with him.

"It's my friend, John," said Charlie.

"It's Doctor Underhill!" said Susan.

[1]**honestly** ehrlich [2]**escape** entkommen

Charlie opened the window and waved to the doctor. The doctor waved to Charlie. "That's right," said Charlie. "My friend, Doctor John Underhill. Let's go down and meet him."

Ten minutes later, Charlie, Susan, David, Karim, Vera, Gillian and Doctor John were in Joe's Snackbar. "Eight milkshakes please, Joe," said Vera.

"So, I think we have found the answer to the secret of the lost dogs," said Gillian. "I don't think those boys will steal any more animals for a long time."

"That's very good news," said Charlie. "Wanda will sleep very well tonight."

"And everybody else, too," said the doctor. "You were great detectives."

COMPREHENSION QUESTIONS

Chapter One

1. When Gillian shot, how many people were there on the football field?
2. Why did the man with the dog drive away very quickly?

Chapter Two

1. How many people were sitting around the big table at Joe's Snackbar?
2. Why do you think there was blood on Flopper's leg?

Chapter Three

1. How did Vera hurt her ankle?
2. Why did some of the children go back to the park?

Chapter Four

1. Why did Charlie bark in Joe's Snackbar?
2. How did the children try to find the owner of Sponker?

Chapter Five

1. Was it easy for the children to find the owner of Sponker?
2. Doctor Underhill told Karim, "How much do you want for Sponker?" What did Doctor Underhill think?

Chapter Six

1. How many samosas did Karim buy?
2. When Mrs. Macintosh brought the cakes and drinks into Charlie's room, what were the children talking about?

Chapter Seven

1. Why was Gillian so excited after having heard what Doctor Underhill had told Charlie?
2. Karim knew Paul Fisher. Why?

Chapter Eight

1. Who brought Flopper back to Mrs. Baxter?
2. Karim led the owner of Bonzo to a house. A woman opened the door. What was her name?

Chapter Nine

1. How did Charlie like his tea? How do you like yours?
2. What animals were in the magician's house?

Chapter Ten

1. Who (or what!) touched the boy's leg?
2. Why did Vera ask Joe for eight milkshakes?

What do you think?

1. In the story there were many different kinds of dog. How many can you remember? Which is your favourite kind of dog? Was it in the story?
2. Is there a dogs' home in your town? Is it a good place to get a dog?
3. Do you like fast food or do you prefer healthy food?
4. David faints when he thinks about blood. Have you ever fainted?
5. Have you ever eaten an Indian samosa? What is it like? If you haven't, turn to page 38.

6. What do you think the police will do with the boys who stole the dogs?
7. What part of the story did you like best?
8. Was there a part of the story that you didn't like?

MAKING SAMOSAS

What you need:

300 g white **flour**[1], 3/4 **tablespoon**[2] salt, 300 g melted butter, 5 tablespoons yoghurt, **minced meat**[3], **red and green peppers**[4], **parsley**[5]

Spices[6]: pepper, **cumin**[7], **turmeric**[8]

How to make the ***dough***[9]*:*

1. **Sift**[10] the flour.
2. Put in the melted butter and **knead**[11].
3. Add the yoghurt and make a thick dough.

How to make the filling:

1. Cook the minced meat in a small **saucepan**[12].
2. Add the **chopped**[13] peppers and parsley.
3. Add the spices.

[1]**flour** Mehl [2]**tablespoon** Esslöffel [3]**minced meat** Hackfleisch [4]**red and green peppers** rote und grüne Paprikaschoten [5]**parsley** Petersilie [6]**spice(s)** Gewürz(e) [7]**cumin** Kreuzkümmel [8]**turmeric** Gelbwurz [9]**dough** Teig [10]**to sift** sieben [11]**to knead** kneten [12]**saucepan** Kochtopf [13]**to chop** zerhacken

How to make the samosas:

1. Roll the dough into small balls. Press them flat. Roll them into very thin **square**[1] pancakes.
2. Cut each pancake in half and fold into a **cone**[2].
3. Put the filling into the cone. Close the **flap**[3] and stick it with a little water.
4. **Deep-fry**[4] the cones in oil (not too many in the **pan**[5]).
5. Take out when **crisp**[6] and dark gold.
6. Serve hot.

[1]**square** viereckig [2]**cone** Kegel [3]**flap** *(hier)* Teiglappen [4]**to deep-fry** frittieren
[5]**pan** Pfanne [6]**crisp** knusprig

987 654 32